Spot the Difference

Leaves

Charlotte Guillain

Heinemann Library
Chicago, Illinois

Customer Service 888-454-2279
Visit our website at www.heinemannraintree.com

Designed by Joanna Hinton-Malivoire
Photo research by Erica Martin and Hannah Taylor
Printed and bound in China by South China Printing Co. Ltd.

12 11 10 09 08
10 9 8 7 6 5 4 3 2 1

Library of Congress Cataloging-in-Publication Data
Guillain, Charlotte.
  Leaves / Charlotte Guillain. -- 1st ed.
      p. cm. -- (Spot the difference)
  Includes index.
  ISBN-13: 978-1-4329-0944-4 (library binding-hardcover)
  ISBN-10: 1-4329-0944-4 (library binding-hardcover)
  ISBN-13: 978-1-4329-0951-2 (pbk.)
  ISBN-10: 1-4329-0951-7 (pbk.)
  1. Leaves--Juvenile literature. I. Title.
  QK649.G85 2008
  581.48-dc22

                                2007035945

Acknowledgements
The publishers would like to thank the following for permission to reproduce photographs: ©FLPA pp. **12**, **22 left**, **23a** (Keith Rushforth), **15**, **23c** (Krystyna Szulecka), **8**, **23b** (M. Szadzuik / R. Zinck), **13**, **23d** (Martin B Withers), **5**, **6** (Nigel Cattlin); ©istockphoto.com pp. **4 bottom right** (Stan Rohrer), **4 top left** (CHEN PING-HUNG), **4 top right** (John Pitcher), **4 bottom left** (Vladimir Ivanov), ©Jonathan Buckley p. **21** (flowerphotos.com); ©Photolibrary pp. **11**, **17**, **18**, **20**, **22 right** (Botanica), **16** (Creatas), **7** (Ifa-Bilderteam Gmbh), **14** (J S Sira), **9** (Kit Young), **19** (Mark Bolton); ©Science Photo Library p. **10** (Bjanka Kadic).

Cover photograph of beech leaves reproduced with permission of ©FLPA (Nigel Cattlin). Back cover photograph of a Swiss cheese plant reproduced with permission of ©FLPA (M. Szadzuik / R. Zinck).

Every effort has been made to contact copyright holders of any material reproduced in this book. Any omissions will be rectified in subsequent printings if notice is given to the publishers.

Contents

What Are Plants?

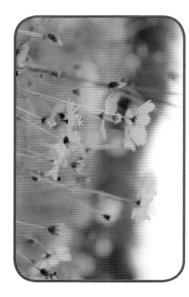

Plants are living things.
Plants live in many places.

Plants need air to grow.
Plants need water to grow.
Plants need sunlight to grow.

What Are Leaves?

Plants have many parts.

roots

stem

leaf

flower

Most plants have leaves.

8

This is a Swiss cheese plant.

Its leaves are smooth.

This is a pussy ears plant.
Its leaves are hairy.

This is a tulip.
It has few leaves.

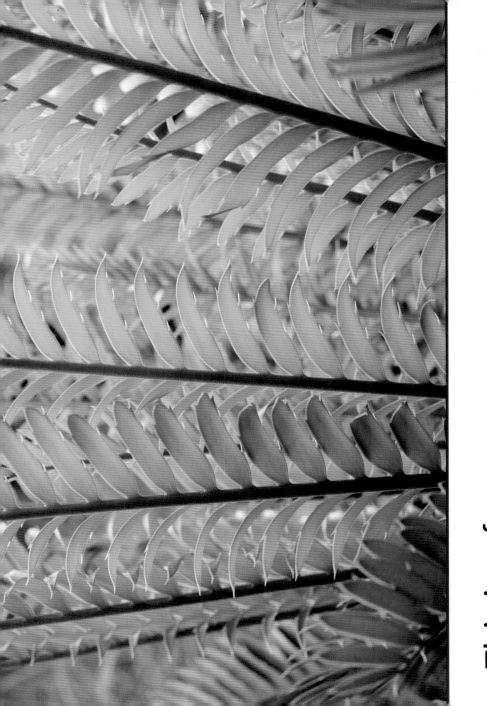

This is a fern.
It has many leaves.

This is a pine tree.
Its leaves are narrow.

This is a banana plant.
Its leaves are wide.

Amazing Leaves

This is a living stone plant.
Its leaves are soft.

This is a monkey puzzle tree.

Its leaves are spiky.

This is a yucca plant.
Its leaves are very long.

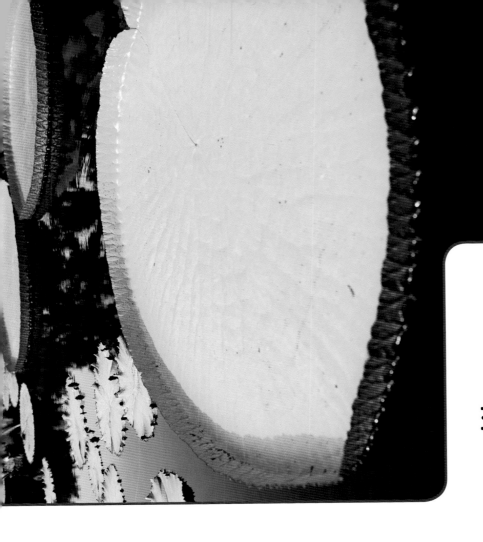

This is a water lily.
Its leaves are very round.

This is a flame nettle.
Its leaves are red.

This is an ivy plant.
Its leaves are yellow.

What Do Leaves Do?

Leaves use sunshine to make plant food.

Leaves help plants grow.

Picture Glossary

narrow close together

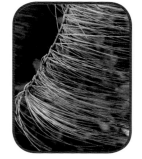

smooth flat; does not have bumps

spiky has sharp points

wide far apart

Index

Note to Parents and Teachers

Before reading
Take in a collection of different leaves from trees and plants. Talk to the children about the different shapes and sizes. Can anyone name what trees the leaves came from? Ask the children to tell you some of the differences between the leaves, such as if they are large or small, rough or smooth, hairy or prickly.

After reading
• Tell the children you are going to quiz them about things they learned in the book. Ask them the following questions: Do most plants have leaves or do most plants not have leaves? Are all leaves the same shape? Are all the leaves the same color? Are all the leaves prickly? How do leaves help the plants?
• Give each child an outline of a leaf made from thin card, such as an oak leaf shape, a maple leaf shape, a holly leaf shape, or a beech leaf shape. Ask them to draw around their template and then to cut out the leaves they have drawn. Help them to stick these onto an appropriate tree outline that you have drawn. Write the name of the tree (using a yellow highlighter) and ask the children to go over your word and to label the leaves.